FUTURE FILES

FUTURE WORLD

A BEGINNER'S GUIDE TO LIFE IN THE 21ST CENTURY

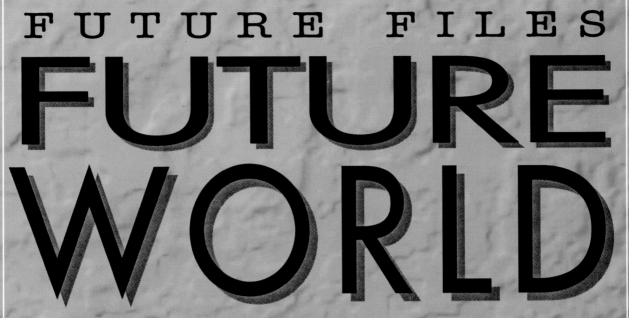

Written by
SARAH ANGLISS
and COLIN UTTLEY
Illustrated by
RICHARD ROCKWOOD
and ALEX PANG

COPPER BEECH BOOKS
BROOKFIELD, CONNECTICUT

© Aladdin Books Ltd 1998

Designed and produced by
Aladdin Books Ltd
28 Percy Street
London W1P 0LD

First published in
the United States in 1998 by
Copper Beech Books,
an imprint of
The Millbrook Press
2 Old New Milford Road
Brookfield, Connecticut 06804

Editor
Simon Beecroft

Design
David West Children's Book Design

Designer Flick Killerby

Picture Research
Brooks Krikler Research

Illustrators
Richard Rockwood and Alex Pang

Series concept
Jim Pipe

Printed in Belgium

Library of Congress Cataloging-in-Publication Data
Angliss, Sarah.
Future world : a beginner's guide to life on earth in the
21st century / by Sarah Angliss and Colin Uttley ;
illustrated by Richard Rockwood and Alex Pang.
p. cm. — (Future files)
Includes index.
Summary: Speculates about what life will be like in the
next century, discussing such topics as population
growth, power sources, architecture, and jobs.
ISBN 0-7613-0821-0 (lib. bdg.). —
ISBN 0-7613-0740-0 (pbk.)
1. Twenty-first century—Forecasts—Juvenile literature.
[1. Twenty-first century—Forecasts.] I. Uttley, Colin.
II. Rockwood, Richard, ill. III. Pang, Alex, ill.
IV. Title. V. Series.
CB161.A57 1998   98-4269
303.49'09'05—dc21   CIP AC

MISSION CONTROL

INTO THE FUTURE

As we enter the new millennium, we are living through a revolution. Astounding new advances in all kinds of technology are changing the way we work, travel, live, and play around the world.

In the middle of this turmoil, it is hard to predict what our cities and homes will be like in a hundred years to come. But this book attempts to imagine our futures, picturing possibilities as it explores some of the most exciting technologies that are emerging for the future.

Two of the greatest agents of change are the computer and the Internet (*see* pages 8-9) — the global network of computers that enables us to exchange information in minutes over any distance. With them comes the development of virtual reality — immersion in a computer world known as cyberspace.

About seven billion people share this planet, and two billion more of us will be here by 2025. As the world's population expands, we will need to find new places to live. Will we build new homes high up in the sky (*see* page 14), underground (*see* pages 12-13), or on the ocean (*see* page 15)?

And what will living in the cities of the future be like? The transportation we use is sure to change (*see* page 17), and our high-tech entertainment may well be dazzling (*see* pages 22-23). But as technology gets ever more advanced, will it create new opportunities for others to snoop into our private lives (*see* pages 26-27)?

This book does not have all the answers. But in the following pages, you can look at where we are today, and look forward to where we may go tomorrow.

Right *Need to tell science fact from science fiction? Take a look at our Reality Check boxes. We can't see into the future, but these cunning devices tell you how realistic an idea is. The more green lights, the better. The "how soon?" line guesses when in the future the idea might become reality: Each green light is 50 years (so in the example here, it's 150 years in the future).*

REALITY CHECK

FEASIBLE TECHNOLOGY	○	○	○	○	○
SCIENCE IS SOUND	○	○	○	○	○
AFFORDABLE	○	○	○	○	○
HOW SOON?	○	○	○	○	○

POWER TO THE PEOPLE

With the population growing even larger, demand for fuel will soon outstrip supply. Global reserves of coal, oil, and gas will run out in the not-too-distant future, so the search is on to provide alternative sources of fuel.

FUEL FOR THE FUTURE

The world once hoped that nuclear power stations would offer endless, cheap electricity. But the disaster at Chernobyl in the former U.S.S.R. showed that nuclear power is costly and can be dangerous. Nuclear waste takes thousands of years to become safe, so new ways of using energy must be developed. Already solar turbines, wind farms, wave machines, and advanced hydroelectric power stations promise renewable (never-ending) supplies of energy.

FUTURE FUSION

Today's nuclear power stations use fission — they smash apart atoms of materials like uranium to release energy. But scientists hope to build commercial fusion reactors soon. These will fuse together atoms of hydrogen to release heat, producing energy in the same way as the stars do.

GASOLINE PROBLEM

In 1973, drivers across the United States stood in line for hours to fill their empty tanks. For the first time, drivers realized that the supply of oil was not unlimited. Since then there has been a revolution in car design. Gone are the large, inefficient cars, replaced by smaller, safer cars with better aerodynamics and small, efficient, "clean" engines. Yet despite the dramatically improved efficiency of cars, there are now more cars on the road than ever before, and oil supplies will soon run out.

MELTDOWN

Remaining toxic for centuries to come, the remains of the nuclear fission reactor at Chernobyl (*right*) have been encased in protective concrete. The disaster at this power station occurred in 1986, when technicians switched off safety systems during an unauthorized test of the reactor. As the temperature in the reactor soared, fuel melted and there was an explosion and a fire, which blew eight tons of deadly nuclear fuel into the atmosphere.

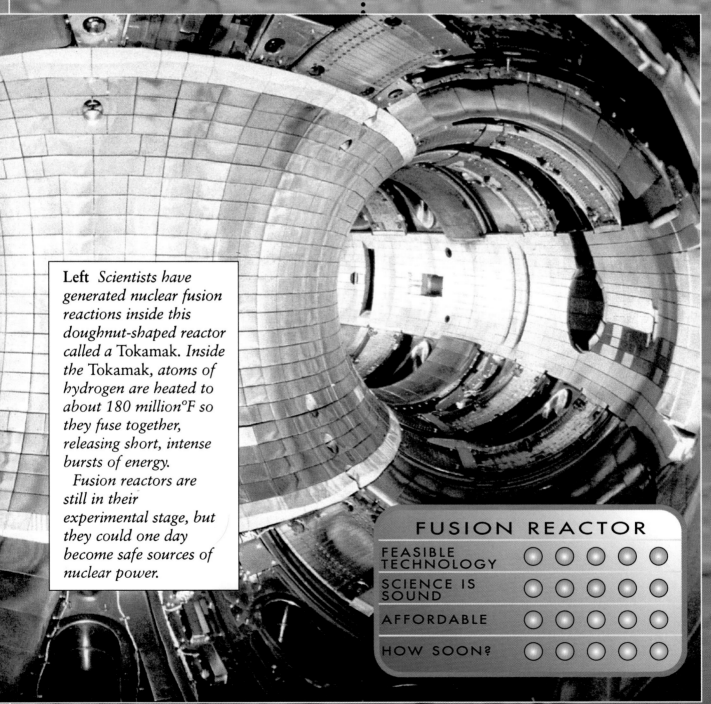

Left *Scientists have generated nuclear fusion reactions inside this doughnut-shaped reactor called a* Tokamak. *Inside the* Tokamak, *atoms of hydrogen are heated to about 180 million°F so they fuse together, releasing short, intense bursts of energy.*

Fusion reactors are still in their experimental stage, but they could one day become safe sources of nuclear power.

FUSION REACTOR

FEASIBLE TECHNOLOGY	○	○	○	○	○
SCIENCE IS SOUND	○	○	○	○	○
AFFORDABLE	○	○	○	○	○
HOW SOON?	○	○	○	○	○

GLOBAL VILLAGE

Technology makes the earth a "global village:" Air travel and satellite pictures have made the world seem smaller — and now, people with a computer and a modem (which links a computer to a telephone line) can contact each other via a vast, global network known as the Internet.

FIBER OPTICS

Today, messages are sent from one computer to another via cables and satellites. Metal wires can only carry a few thousand messages at once. They are being replaced by fiber-optic links, fine strands of glass that can carry far more. Words, sounds, and pictures from your computer will then be converted into pulses of light and beamed along these cables faster than ever before.

Left Dedicated Internet users today hardly ever leave their computers. But in the 1995 film Johnny Mnemonic, *a cybersurfer is chased through a virtual, on-line world* (see *page* 22).

CAFE SOCIETY

A place where you can surf the Internet for an hour or so, the "cybercafe" hit the headlines when the Internet first became a household name in the 1990s. It made Internet surfing into a social activity. But as more people set up connections to the Web from their own homes, surfing is becoming a solo activity.

IN TOUCH

It looks like we're going to spend a lot more time on-line. So it's no surprise that we would like to be able to see, hear, and feel each other over the Internet. A device called a "dataglove" can already give us the sensation of touching on-line. Still unrefined, it cannot yet simulate the feedback you feel when forcing another object to move.

Below *Covered with a network of fine tubes, datagloves fill with air to create the sensation of something in your hand.*

NOT FOR EVERYONE

Not everyone can enjoy the neighborliness of the global village. While many of us are better connected than ever before, a third of the planet will never get the chance to make a telephone call in their lives. The world may soon be divided into the "information rich" and the "information poor" — those with high-tech computers and those without. Those without a home on the Internet may feel more isolated than ever before.

Above *Fluctuations in the Tokyo Stock Exchange early in 1998 caused aftershocks around the whole of the planet. High-speed data links mean we now live in a close-knit global economy. A century ago, traders took days to exchange money with a neighboring city. Today, they can move it to the other side of the world in seconds.*

HIGH-TECH DATAGLOVES

FEASIBLE TECHNOLOGY	●	●	●	●	●
SCIENCE IS SOUND	●	●	●	●	●
AFFORDABLE	●	●	●	●	○
HOW SOON?	●	●	●	●	○

THINKING BUILDINGS

Half the world's energy supply is used to power buildings. As the cost of energy increases and supplies of fossil fuels run out, architects are looking for new ways to run our homes and offices. Abandoning energy-hungry heating and cooling systems, they're going back to the drawing board, looking for new building designs that can make the most of the elements. They're also adding "intelligence" to the buildings they create so they can make the most of wind, air, and sunlight.

Left *Air speeds up as it passes between the two towers of Tomigaya II, powering a giant wind turbine that generates the building's electricity.*

TOMIGAYA II

Architect Richard Rogers has used the aerodynamics of a skyscraper to tap a source of clean energy. Planned for Tokyo, Japan, the Tomigaya II is a twin skyscraper that is shaped to accelerate the air around it. A pleasant place to live and work, Tomigaya II also has a deep basement that stays moderately cool throughout the year. This helps it to regulate its temperature without using air conditioning.

AN EYE TO THE WEATHER

The outside walls of the Institute of the Arab World in Paris (*above*) are constantly changing, like a living organism. This building is covered in mechanical irises, devices that open and close as the light levels change. They keep the building at a steady temperature, helping to conserve the precious artifacts inside.

CRAZY HOUSE

Holding its owner captive, the switched-on house in the 1977 movie *Demon Seed* made movie-goers uneasy about the idea of "intelligent" buildings. But in reality, intelligence is designed to make our homes more comfortable.

Left *The Green Building is a proposal for an office that would suck fresh air into its central space and push stale air out of its top. The main intelligence comes from the residents themselves. They use windows and mirrors to control the levels of heat and light.*

THINKING BUILDINGS

FEASIBLE TECHNOLOGY	○ ○ ○ ○ ○
SCIENCE IS SOUND	○ ○ ○ ○ ○
AFFORDABLE	○ ○ ○ ○ ○
HOW SOON?	○ ○ ○ ○ ○

TALL ORDER

The Hong Kong and Shanghai Bank (above), completed in 1986, towers 590 ft above Hong Kong. Computer-controlled mirrors on the top relfect sunlight through the middle of the building to lower levels (left). To be completed in 2001, the Shanghai World Financial Center in Pudong, China's new financial district, will be brimmng with intelligence, including a computer system that reduces its sway during an earthquake.

INTO THE EARTH ·

As the population of our cities grows (*below*), the price of land is at a premium. Unable to afford to build at street level, many city dwellers are contemplating a future undground.

UNDERGROUND CITY

The Kumagai Corporation of Japan has already unveiled plans for an ambitious new underground complex (*far right*). Deep below the streets of Tokyo, it will have shops, cafes, and homes. Air will be recycled to keep it fresh. Ultraviolet lights will flood the streets, helping plants to grow. Massive video screens will relay pictures of the outside world to make people feel comfortable in their new environment — but will people be able to adjust?

Left *The people of Matmata, Tunisia, made their homes below the soft rock centuries ago.*
Below *Cool, comfortable hotels in Turkey have now been built underground.*

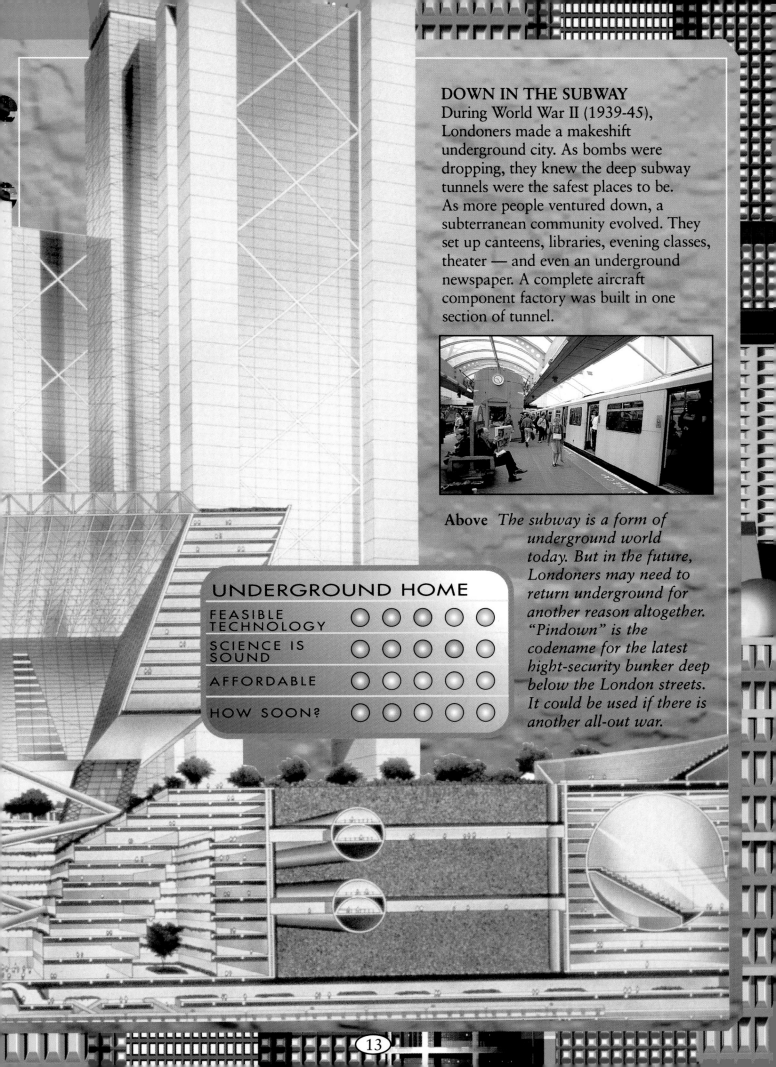

DOWN IN THE SUBWAY

During World War II (1939-45), Londoners made a makeshift underground city. As bombs were dropping, they knew the deep subway tunnels were the safest places to be. As more people ventured down, a subterranean community evolved. They set up canteens, libraries, evening classes, theater — and even an underground newspaper. A complete aircraft component factory was built in one section of tunnel.

Above *The subway is a form of underground world today. But in the future, Londoners may need to return underground for another reason altogether. "Pindown" is the codename for the latest hight-security bunker deep below the London streets. It could be used if there is another all-out war.*

UNDERGROUND HOME

FEASIBLE TECHNOLOGY	○	○	○	○	○
SCIENCE IS SOUND	○	○	○	○	○
AFFORDABLE	○	○	○	○	○
HOW SOON?	○	○	○	○	○

LIVING OFF THE GROUND

Tomorrow's skyscraper could house a million people. Dwarfing today's multistory buildings, projects like X-Seed 4000 are taking the concept of the high-rise to a new extreme.

X-SEED 4000

In the past we have built skyward when overcrowding has been a problem. Still on the drawing board, X-Seed 4000 is a space-saving skyscraper that the Taisei Construction Company has proposed for Japan. A massive grid of lightweight steel, it will tower almost 2½ miles into the sky.

BIG IDEA

X-Seed 4000 is designed for living in. But with a snow-covered peak, it can also be used for winter sports and research into weather. Magnetic elevators will carry people around this structure, whisking them to the top in just 30 minutes. This project was first proposed in the 1980s, but one day people may need to begin building such a monster.

Left Proposed by the writer Arthur C. Clarke in the 1950s, this satellite home would be tethered to Earth. Supplies would be sent along the tether. People would reach it this way too — on an amazing elevator ride.

Below The film Waterworld *shows an Earth that's swamped by water. With no land to make their home, survivors live on boats or floating shantytowns.*

HIGH IDEALS

Calling them "machines for living," Swiss architect Le Corbusier built ultra-modern, functional houses from the latest materials. He boxed them together to make cities in the sky — high-rise buildings like his Unité d'Habitation in Marseilles, France (right). Le Corbusier's sky cities were successful, but those built by his imitators were often drab. The 1960s housing projects dampened the enthusiasm for high-rise living.

Below Spinning to produce artificial gravity, the space station is the ultimate in high living. Giant space stations could have all the facilities of a large town, leaving little need to return to Earth.

SATELLITE CITIES

FEASIBLE TECHNOLOGY	○	●	●	●	○
SCIENCE IS SOUND	○	●	●	●	●
AFFORDABLE	○	●	●	●	○
HOW SOON?	○	○	●	●	○

Above *Floating in the ocean like a giant iceberg, most of Marinopolis would be below the water. Proposed by Japan's Kajima Corporation, this sea city tackles more than overcrowding. In a country that suffers from earthquakes, the water would cushion its buildings from shock waves, making them far less likely to collapse.*

END OF THE ROAD? • Transportation without gas

The car has become the slowest way to travel through our cities. Noisy, dirty, and slow, cars will be replaced in city centers by efficient, eco-friendly transportation.

ON THE MOVE

People movers have been constructed in several cities in the United States, such as Miami and Detroit. These driverless electric trains travel at low speeds along a continuous circuit. People can just step on and off from platforms spaced at regular intervals.

Cars of the future will have fuel-efficient, low-emisson engines, and may use cells powered by the sun (solar power), or even be powered by hydrogen (*see* page 17).

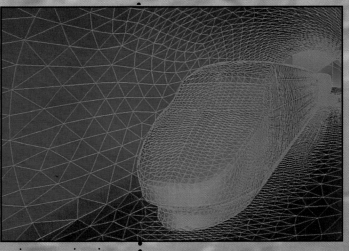

Left Just the thing for traveling between cities, high-speed trains can get there faster than cars. Trains can cruise at almost 200 miles per hour if the tracks have up-to-date computerized signaling.

ON AUTOMATIC

Driving may get easier if congestion gets worse — because we may have to rely on the "intelligent" car. Using sensors to check its speed and position, this may be a lifesaver in crowded, fast-moving traffic. With their route guided by a global positioning satellite, passengers only need to worry about the in-car entertainment.

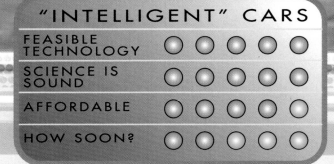

"INTELLIGENT" CARS

FEASIBLE TECHNOLOGY	○	○	○	○	○
SCIENCE IS SOUND	○	○	○	○	○
AFFORDABLE	○	○	○	○	○
HOW SOON?	○	○	○	○	○

TAKING A BREATHER

Heavy traffic in our cities leaves millions of people choking in smog. Polluted Los Angeles opened oxygen shops in the 1970s. Customers could use them for a breath of fresh air when they needed a break from the fumes in the street.

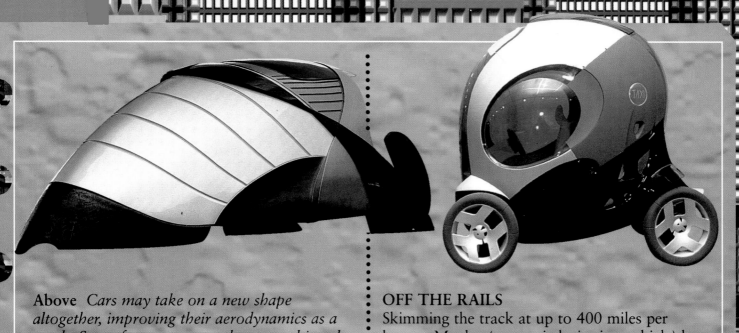

Above *Cars may take on a new shape altogether, improving their aerodynamics as a result. Some future cars may be covered in solar panels so they can be powered by the sun.*

CLEAN MACHINE

Cars powered by hydrogen gas — a good fuel — have already been built, but new developments will use the sun's energy to "crack" water, releasing hydrogen from water. Hydrogen doesn't produce harmful fumes. Better still, if it leaks into the air, this fuel will make it cleaner — clearing away dust particles that cause pollution.

OFF THE RAILS

Skimming the track at up to 400 miles per hour, a Maglev (magnetic levitation vehicle) has no moving parts, but is propelled by a linear motor. This creates a magnetic field that varies along the track, lifting the vehicle and pushing it along (*below*). Smooth, quiet, and efficient, Maglevs are already running commercially in Japan. Advances in "superconductors," materials that offer no resistance to electricity, could bring down the cost of running linear motors. This would make Maglevs one of the cheapest, cleanest rides around.

Right *Cars in the 1982 film* Blade Runner *have taken to the air. This sci-fi classic is set in 2019, in a Los Angeles that's overrun with traffic. Computers control the airborne traffic to avoid any crashes. The roads themselves are used by pedestrians.*

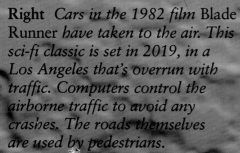

JOB SHIFT •
The future of work

Machines like cars and printing presses have already replaced much of the physical effort of humans. Soon, robots with computer brains may replace some of our thinking power. Sharpness of mind could matter more than strength and dexterity as we compete with intelligent machines.

ON-LINE OFFICES

In the future, technologies like the Internet will enable us to exchange ideas faster than ever. They're already changing the places where we work — labor-intensive typing pools (*above*) have already become a thing of the past.

HOME WORK

An on-line discussion can take place in a "telesuite" (*above*). In this new type of meeting room, business people can join co-workers from around the world without ever leaving their offices. Meanwhile, e-mail (electronic messages sent over the Internet) helps millions of people to keep in touch with their offices while working in their own homes (*below left*).

MODEL MAKERS

Computer design systems enable designers to draft their ideas in three dimensions — with no need for an old-fashioned drawing board. By wearing virtual-reality headsets (see page 22) they can even "walk around" their new designs.

TAILOR-MADE

The robot production line (*below*) brought the world identical, affordable goods, but the next manufacturing revolution will allow us to have cheap items made to order. Using a system called "near net processing," smart robots can take commands directly from the sales department. They can sculpt a one-of-a-kind item for a customer, adapting it to his or her requirements. Before long, your favorite store may be able to make you an outfit with a perfect fit, matching it to your own measurements. High-tech car plants can already produce single cars with the color, trimmings, and extras to order. Textile companies can produce short runs of fabrics with customized patterns.

Above *Cutting and baling hay, this decision-making robot farmer finds the most efficient way to clear a field.*

Below *After finding a vehicle's gas tank, these high-tech robots can fill it up. In places where safety and accuracy are critical, it may be smart to use a robot stand-in. Clean cars of the future may be powered by the gas hydrogen (see page 17). As this can be hazardous for humans to handle, this fuel could be delivered by robot attendants.*

ROBOT WORKERS

FEASIBLE TECHNOLOGY	○	○	○	○	○
SCIENCE IS SOUND	○	○	○	○	○
AFFORDABLE	○	○	○	○	○
HOW SOON?	○	○	○	○	○

SMART MONEY •

In the future, you won't need to check to see if you have your cash, keys, and credit cards. Already on trial in several cities around the world, the smart card (*right*) will be the holder of tomorrow's money.

INTELLIGENT PLASTIC

The smart card may look like an ordinary bank card, but that's where the similarity ends. Embedded in its surface is a rugged microchip that can hold vast amounts of personal data — your bank account details, your medical record, and even the access code for your front door. Swiping your smart card through a reader will enable you to pay for goods, identify yourself, and open doors in the future.

SILICON SLUMP

Wiping out a trillion dollars around the world, the stock market crash of 1987 was a setback caused partly by on-line trading. When share prices started falling, computer systems automatically started selling shares at ever-lower prices. The crash showed that using computers to run the world's complex money systems can have its dangers.

Below *Don't send a check — punch those numbers. This keypad has a built-in card reader to let smart-card users exchange funds with each other.*

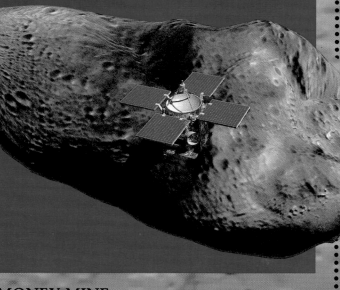

MONEY MINE

Cash may be going out of date, but the way we value goods hasn't changed for centuries. We still base some prices on the cost of rare materials. Asteroids contain abundant supplies of metals that are rare on earth, like platinum; if one were captured and mined for its resources (*above*), it could turn the world economy upside down.

FACE THE FUTURE

Detecting the temperature contours of the face, this "thermogram" (*left*) creates an image that is unique to every one of us. The best thermograms can even tell identical twins apart. Banks and stores may soon be using a technology like this to identify their customers at cash machines and cash registers. They have already trialed fingerprint matchers and low-powered lasers that scan the retina of the eye (*below*). The ultimate identifier, which uses a state-of-the-art polymer, reads the traces of DNA left by a user's fingerprint.

HIGH-TECH CASH MACHINES

FEASIBLE TECHNOLOGY	○	○	○	○	○
SCIENCE IS SOUND	○	○	○	○	○
AFFORDABLE	○	○	○	○	
HOW SOON?	○	○	○	○	

TIME OUT • A future that is *serious* fun

Computers are set to change the way we play. We may spend more of our leisure time in cyberspace — the artificial world of the computer. "Virtual-reality," now in its infancy, uses computers to give us the impression that we have entered a three-dimensional world — wearing a special headset, we can "walk around" environments that exist only in the computer.

ONLY ON PAPER

Unlike a CD-ROM or computer game, you can take books and words on paper anywhere. But researchers at Xerox are developing a rival for the printed page — virtual paper. It looks like ordinary paper, but if you magnified the surface, you would see it was made up of tiny balls, which are white on one side and black on the other. As you "write" on the page, the balls turn over, from white to black, so your words appear. By connecting the page to a computer, you could then send a personalized message in your own handwriting via the Internet.

Above *Technology gets rid of some of the undesirable elements of the real world — there's no bad weather at this state-of-the-art artificial beach in Japan, called Ocean Dome.*

GET REAL

Most cartoon characters are animated using thousands of separate pictures. But some modern movies, like *Lawnmower Man II* (*left*), use computers to animate characters. Even short sequences of digital special effects like these can take hours of computing time to do. But computers are doubling in speed every decade. In the future, movies with digital characters will be produced as quickly as ones with live actors.

VIRTUAL PAPER

FEASIBLE TECHNOLOGY	○	○	○	○	○
SCIENCE IS SOUND	○	○	○	○	○
AFFORDABLE	○	○	○	○	○
HOW SOON?	○	○	○	○	

Left
Following every move of the player's hand, this advanced robot by Toshiba can play a perfect game of beach volleyball. The speed of its volleys can be controlled to match the player's own skill.

VIRTUALLY THERE

Today's theme parks are made of bricks and mortar, but the vacation destinations of tomorrow could exist in cyberspace (an imaginary world created by a computer). Designers of the future could study the world's treasures, then create idealized copies of them in a virtual domain. For example, we could visit the Great Pyramids of Egypt by plugging into our computers — and enjoy a real-life journey into the lives of the pharaohs.

CLEAN ACT

Virtual destinations could be cleaned up to suit the inexperienced traveler — they could be made just like new, and with fewer other tourists. Some could be fantasy locations, like the legendary Lost City of Atlantis. Others could take visitors on a whistle-stop tour of locations beyond the planet.

Favorite real-world destinations, like Egypt and Venice, are already buckling under the strain of mass tourism. The rise of cheap global travel means these sights may be damaged for good. Though it would not be the same as the real thing, virtual travel could help to save precious sites — or it could take away the incentive to care for them at all.

Above *Future vacation companies may employ technicians to design "perfect" locations that people can visit virtually.*

Below *Wired to a virtual reality system, a future "cybertourist" takes a journey around the perfectly conserved Great Pyramids in Egypt. In reality the monuments may be slowly turning to rubble (right). For generations to come, virtual copies may be all that we have of the world's treasured sights.*

FAULTY START

Today's virtual reality is a clumsy affair. Users must wear a heavy visor and thick datagloves (see page 9) to immerse themselves in cyberspace. Engineers are already experimenting with lightweight systems that use laser beams to scan images directly onto the retina of the eye. For the ultimate virtual-reality experience, they propose plugging a system directly into the sensory areas of the brain.

Below *The hero of the film* Johnny Mnemonic *(1995) experiences a world of virtual cities. But it is likely that virtual reality will become a part of our everyday lives. Home-shopping by phone or computer is already possible. But virtual supermarkets could let us wander the aisles and pick up the products before we choose what to buy.*

VIRTUAL VACATIONS

FEASIBLE TECHNOLOGY	○	○	○	○	○
SCIENCE IS SOUND	○	○	○	○	○
AFFORDABLE	○	○	○	○	○
HOW SOON?	○	○	○	○	○

BIG BROTHER •  Snooping in cyberspace

Cyberspace is not safe. Every time you send an e-mail, or surf the Internet, you could be watched. Laws prevent ordinary citizens from tapping into your private communications, but governments could become digital snoops (*right*).

COMPUTER SPIES

Years ago, you needed expert wire tappers or marked notes to keep an eye on someone from a distance. But all you need now is access to the computers your suspect relies on.

ON THE WIRE

We're surprisingly tolerant of the official snoops. We shop in stores that use video cameras, work in offices that monitor our computer use, and answer detailed personal questions on government forms. But when, in 1997, the U.S. government tried to outlaw some "encryption" software (which enables people to keep the contents of their e-mails to themselves), computer users fought back — the government had snooped too far.

DATA THIEVES

As organizations store more information on-line, computer hacking (illegally connecting to other people's computers) has become a bigger security threat than ever. Movie studio MGM claims their own website was hacked into while it was advertising the film Hackers *(right). Many hackers consider themselves to be harmless pranksters, but a minority are more malicious — blackmailing companies, reading personal files, and planting computer viruses on their victims.*

KEEPING TRACK

Police tracing the movements of a criminal are helped by the data they can gather from banks, stores, and telephone companies (*right*). But some people are concerned that personal data could be collected without our knowledge or permission.

Above *Some computers today can be operated by voice commands. The next generation will recognize the voices of particular users, improving security.*

Right *Ray Bradbury's fantasy,
Fahrenheit 451, shows a
future society whose
leaders banned
books — they
are burned by
"firemen."*

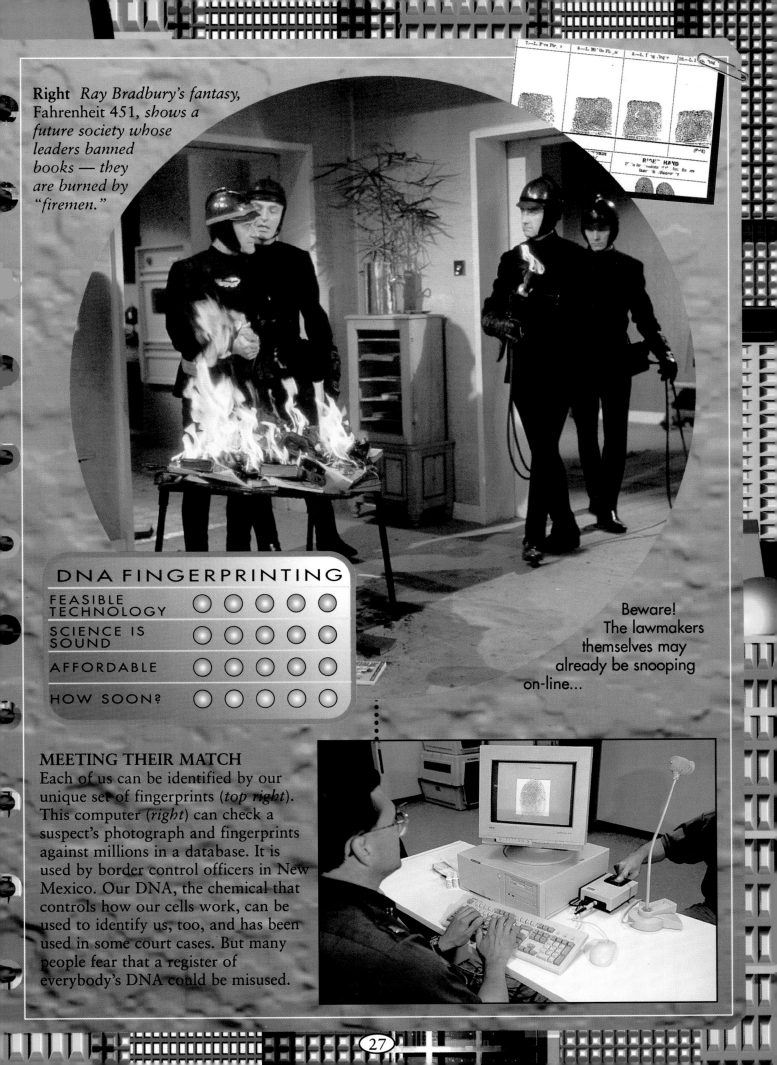

DNA FINGERPRINTING

FEASIBLE TECHNOLOGY	●	●	●	●	●
SCIENCE IS SOUND	●	●	●	●	●
AFFORDABLE	●	●	●	●	●
HOW SOON?	●	●	●	●	●

Beware!
The lawmakers
themselves may
already be snooping
on-line...

MEETING THEIR MATCH

Each of us can be identified by our
unique set of fingerprints (*top right*).
This computer (*right*) can check a
suspect's photograph and fingerprints
against millions in a database. It is
used by border control officers in New
Mexico. Our DNA, the chemical that
controls how our cells work, can be
used to identify us, too, and has been
used in some court cases. But many
people fear that a register of
everybody's DNA could be misused.

A CLASS APART · Will technology benefit us all?

Technology is a force for improving our quality of life, but some new technologies are wildly expensive, at least at first. So how soon will it be before everybody benefits?

Left *With makeshift shelters and poor sanitation, a shantytown grows at the fringes of a city. Will its population be able to afford future technology?*

KEEPING IN TOUCH
The telephone used to be thought of as a luxury. Now it is essential, even a lifesaver. Yet not everyone can pay their telephone bill. The videophone (which lets us see as well as hear the person at the other end of the line) may well take over as a means of staying in touch with others — but will everyone be able to afford it? As the pace of change quickens, is it possible to ensure that some people are not excluded from the high-tech world (*below*)?

IDEAL HOMES?
Don't be fooled by these quaint buildings (*above*) — this is Celebration, Disney's city for tomorrow. Walt Disney's first design for a high-tech city was EPCOT (the Experimental Prototype Community of Tomorrow), a futuristic funfair (*see page 29*). But with its old-style charm, Celebration attempts to turn the clock back for its wealthy residents. The city is sealed off from the outside world — only its carefully chosen residents can enter. In this way, uncomfortable realities like crime, poverty, and messy streets can be ignored.

GENETIC THERAPY

FEASIBLE TECHNOLOGY	●	●	●	●	●
SCIENCE IS SOUND	●	●	●	●	○
AFFORDABLE	●	●	●	●	○
HOW SOON?	●	●	●	○	○

FASHION GENES

Some wealthy people choose to go under the surgeon's knife when they want to improve their looks. But cosmetic surgery could become a thing of the past if genetic therapies develop. Genetic therapy involves altering our genes — the chemicals in our bodies responsible for characteristics like sex, height, and hair color. A therapy that slows down ageing, for instance, would be a very popular commodity.

DIVIDED FUTURE

Technology can benefit some people more than others, For example, computers could let the wealthy work from their homes, leaving the urban sprawl for a disadvantaged majority. Expensive genetic therapies (*see* above) could make certain groups of people fitter, stronger, even taller, than the rest of us — perhaps enabling them to develop into a distinct species. Written in 1895, H.G. Wells' *The Time Machine* warns us about this. Its technically-superior Morlocks live in underground cities, preying on the disadvantaged Eloi, who scrape a living on the surface. Let's hope we will use technology in a way that helps us all, making a future world that every one of us can celebrate.

Below *Unlike its futuristic transportation ideas, EPCOT's ideals seem antiquated. For example, Disney wanted it to welcome only the "right type" of person.*

GLOSSARY

AERODYNAMICS
The science of airflow; in particular, how easily vehicles move through air or water.

ASTEROID
A lump of rock, usually less than a mile in diameter, that orbits the sun. Most asteroids orbit between the planets Mars and Jupiter in the Asteroid Belt.

CHERNOBYL
The site of a nuclear (fission) power station in the former U.S.S.R. A reactor at Chernobyl went into meltdown (when the fuel in the reactor overheats and melts through its insulation) on April 26th, 1986, releasing eight tons of deadly radioactive materials into the atmosphere.

CYBER
Refers to computers and machines that are controlled by computers.

CYBERCAFE
A cafe where people eat and drink as well as hire computer terminals connected to the Internet.

CYBERSPACE
A computer-generated artificial world. Someone who plays a virtual reality game is in cyberspace.

CYBERSURFER
Someone who spends time in cyberspace, for example on the Internet.

DATA
Any kind of information, for example the words, pictures, and sounds that are stored on the Internet.

DATAGLOVE
A device that gives you the sensation of touching someone over a computer network, such as the Internet.

DEOXYRIBONUCLEIC ACID (DNA)
The chain of molecules in the heart of every one of the cells that make up your body. Your DNA controls how your body works, and is unique to you.

ECO-FRIENDLY
Term used to describe something that does not harm the environment, for example a fuel that does not pollute the air.

E-MAIL
Electronic mail — messages sent from one computer to another over the Internet instead of by ordinary mail.

ENCRYPTION SOFTWARE
Computer software that enables you to put information, such as personal e-mails, into a secret code. Only you and the person you wish to receive your message should have the software needed to decode it.

EPCOT
The Experimental Prototype Community of Tomorrow, at Disney World in Florida, is based on Walt Disney's vision of a high-tech futuristic city.

FISSION REACTOR
A nuclear reactor that breaks apart heavy atoms, such as atoms of uranium or plutonium, releasing energy and stray particles. There are fission reactors in nuclear power stations today.

FUSION REACTOR
A nuclear reactor that forces lightweight atoms together, such as atoms of hydrogen, releasing a huge burst of energy and stray particles.

GLOBAL POSITIONING SATELLITE
One of a number of satellites that orbit the Earth, forming a worldwide navigation system used by vehicles on sea, land, or in the air. By receiving signals from three of these satellites, vehicles can find their location.

HACKERS
People who break into other people's computers, usually to look at the data that's stored on them.

INTELLIGENCE
The ability of some machines to make certain decisions for themselves, such as opening and closing windows to control temperature changes.

INTELLIGENT BUILDINGS
Buildings that contain computers or other systems that help them to function in the best way possible, for instance to make better use of the sun's heat.

INTERNET
A vast network of computers that we can use to send words, pictures, sounds, and moving images around the world.

LINEAR MOTOR
A type of motor that is in the shape of a long track. A linear motor creates a varying magnetic field that can be used to propel things forward.

MAGLEV
A magnetic levitation vehicle — a train-like vehicle that moves and hovers above a linear motor that acts as its rails.

NEAR NET PROCESSING
A manufacturing method that allows machines on a production line to produce one-of-a-kind copies of an object, such as a car or clothing.

ON-LINE
A computer or person is "on-line" if they are connected to a network, such as the Internet.

SMART
A computer-related term for advanced technology.

SMART CARD
A slim, plastic card with an embedded microchip that can hold vast amounts of data.

SOLAR PANELS
Panels that can capture energy from the sun and use it to generate electricity.

SURFER
Someone who uses the Internet.

TELESUITE
A room where people can "meet" but aren't there in person but who are connected over the Internet.

TURBINE
A motor containing a shaft fitted with blades that is turned by a liquid or a gas.

VIRTUAL PAPER
A sheet of paper that can be wiped clean and used again as easily as a computer screen.

VIRTUAL REALITY
A computer-generated imaginary world that gives the illusion of being three-dimensional and in which a user is completely immersed.

WEB
An everyday term for the place where information is stored on the Internet. This word is short for "Worldwide Web."

INDEX

PHOTO CREDITS
Abbreviations: t-*top*,
m-*middle*, b-*bottom*,
r-*right*, l-*left*, c-*center*
Cover ml – Columbia/
Tristar (courtesy Kobal).
Cover mr & b, 6-7, 9b, 12-13,
14b, 15, 16t, 22tr & b, 21-22, 25m &
b, 27b, 28t & b & back cover – Frank
Spooner Pictures. 6bl, 8b, 9t, 10ml,
11b, 12b, 17tl & tr, 18t & br, 19tr &
b, 20tr, 25t, 26b, 28m & 29 – Rex
Features. 7t – AEA Technology. 8t –
Twentieth Century Fox (courtesy
Kobal). 10mr & 36m – Kobal
Collection. 11c, 12tl & 18bl – Pictor
International. 13 & 22l – Roger
Vlitos. 14m – Universal Pictures (cour-
tesy Kobal). 17b – Ladd Co./Warner
Bros (courtesy Kobal). 19tl – Rover
UK. 20tl & b – National Westminster
Bank. 22t – First Independent (cour-
tesy Kobal). 27t – Anglo
Enterprizes/Vineyard (courtesy Kobal).